Lerner **SPORTS**

···ESPORTS···
CHAMPIONSHIPS

Heather E. Schwartz

Lerner Publications ◆ Minneapolis

SPORTS THRILLS *MEET* RESEARCH SKILLS

Lerner SPORTS

Free Database Trial: **lernersports.com**

Lerner Publications Company
An imprint of Lerner Publishing Group, Inc.
241 First Avenue North
Minneapolis, MN 55401 USA

For reading levels and more information, look up this title at www.lernerbooks.com.

Main body text set in Aptifer Sans LT Pro. Typeface provided by Linotype AG.

Designer: Viet Chu **Photo Editor:** Annie Zheng

Library of Congress Cataloging-in-Publication Data

Names: Schwartz, Heather E. author.
Title: Esports championships / Heather E. Schwartz.
Description: Minneapolis, MN : Lerner Publications, [2024] | Series: Esports zone | Includes bibliographical
    references and index. | Audience: Ages 7–11 | Audience: Grades 2–3 | Summary: "The biggest esports
    championship events draw in big crowds and award huge prizes to winners. Find out what it takes to win
    esports championships at the amateur, college, and pro levels"— Provided by publisher.
Identifiers: LCCN 2022038705 (print) | LCCN 2022038706 (ebook) | ISBN 9781728490885 (library binding) |
    ISBN 9798765602911 (paperback) | ISBN 9781728497426 (ebook)
Subjects: LCSH: eSports (Contests)—Juvenile literature.
Classification: LCC GV1469.34.E86 S35 2024 (print) | LCC GV1469.34.E86 (ebook) | DDC 794.8—dc23/
    eng/202209215

LC record available at https://lccn.loc.gov/2022038705
LC ebook record available at https://lccn.loc.gov/2022038706

Manufactured in the United States of America
1-53019-51037-12/15/2022

TABLE OF CONTENTS

INTRODUCTION
ESPORTS ENERGY

In July 2022, gamers from all around the world flocked to Raleigh, North Carolina. Inside the PNC Arena, fans waved flags and screamed from the stands. They were eager to see players compete in the *Apex Legends* Global Series Championship.

Fans kept their eyes on the arena's video board and two giant screens. They wanted their favorite *Apex Legends* teams to claim victory and some of the $2 million prize money. Many more fans streamed the event online. They created energy and excitement for the arena's first esports event.

Big events raise the stakes for gamers. In esports, gamers challenge themselves and other players. Their hard work pays off when they level up, improve their play, and win events and tournaments.

Fast Facts

- By 2025, experts predict esports viewers will total more than three hundred million fans.

- Esports are most popular in the US, China, South Korea, Sweden, and Denmark.

- The largest esports tournament prize pool so far was more than $40 million.

- Toronto Esports Arena in Canada is one of the largest esports arenas in the world.

CHAPTER 1

ESPORTS EXPLAINED

IF YOU ASK SOMEONE TO NAME A FEW COMMON SPORTS, THEY'D PROBABLY COME UP WITH SUCH GAMES AS BASEBALL AND SOCCER. Esports are in a category all their own. They don't require running, dribbling, or skating. Gamers don't need to be tall or have big muscles to succeed in esports. In some ways, they're more like activities that rely on brain power, such as playing chess and competing in spelling bees.

Some video games tap into both physical and mental skills. *Fortnite* and *League of Legends*, for example, require quick reflexes and muscle memory for best results. In esports, gamers get to compete against real people, just as athletes in other sports do. Gamers enjoy testing their moves and skills against the talents of other esports athletes.

People play video games on phones, consoles, and personal computers.

While esports have a few things in common with other sports, there's one major difference. Most sports take place in the real world. Players have to travel to the same place, such as a field or a swimming pool, to compete against one another. But esports are virtual. Players can take part from wherever they live, even if they're thousands of miles apart. That makes esports easier for almost everyone to play.

People of all ages can play video games.

Esports are more inclusive than sports that require physical strength. Many sports separate male and female players. In esports, people of different genders can usually play in the same events.

Women and men compete with one another at an esports event.

ESPORTS FOR ALL

Tucker Griggs has been unable to move the joints in his arms and legs since he was born. He uses his feet for everything from cooking and cleaning to esports. He's a top-ranked *Overwatch* player.

Hundreds of fans watch gamers compete at an esports event in 2019.

Esports are growing fast around the world, so it's no surprise they've created a billion-dollar industry. Online tournaments rake in money by streaming events and selling tickets, gear, and ads. They also offer plenty of prize money to superstar players.

Big cash prizes make the drama of esports events even more exciting. That's one reason why experts predict esports viewers will total more than three hundred million by 2025. Fans show up in person and tune in all around the world. The US, China, South Korea, Sweden, and Denmark have the biggest esports fan bases. People are eager to watch what happens when top players face off for esports' biggest prizes.

A woman streams an esports event on her phone.

WANT TO COMPETE IN ESPORTS AS A PRO GAMER? Getting there starts with focus. Maybe you're into strategy games such as *Hearthstone*. Perhaps you prefer creative games such as *Roblox*. Each type of game has something to offer. But when you have big gaming goals, it makes sense to focus on your favorite game.

Pro gamers spend a lot of time practicing to improve their play. Some spend twelve to fourteen hours a day playing video games. They play six days a week. They also watch other gamers online and pick up tips from guides and fellow players.

Learning from fellow gamers is one of the best ways to improve at esports.

Practicing all day is one way to master a video game, but it's not a good idea. Spending too much time looking at a screen isn't healthy. Pro esports players often burn out. They become worn down from the long practice hours. They get injured from performing the same hand and wrist movements over and over. Their mental health suffers too. Without time to relax with friends and family, they can get stressed and depressed.

Staring at screens for too long can cause eyestrain. People with eyestrain may have sore eyes, headaches, and blurry vision.

Playing physical sports such as basketball can help keep our minds and bodies healthy.

To be a successful gamer, follow a more balanced plan. Even if gaming is your favorite thing to do, limit your daily screen time. That way, you'll be healthier and happier, and you can keep gaming for years to come.

CHAPTER 3
GEARING UP

HAVING THE RIGHT GEAR IS ANOTHER WAY GAMERS HELP THEMSELVES SUCCEED. In other sports, athletes might use such equipment as sticks, bats, and gloves. Esports players need good gear too. That includes laptops, keyboards, screens, gaming chairs, speakers, and other equipment. They also need internet access.

Gear can be expensive. But gamers don't have to purchase everything at once to compete in esports. And they don't have to buy only the best equipment. Many gamers level up their gear slowly, one item at a time. Each improvement might lead to better game play. They might also find that the best gear doesn't always come at the highest price.

Gamers wear headsets to communicate with one another during events.

Many gamers don't want to compete in esports. They play video games to relax and have fun with their friends.

Gamers usually start playing alone or with friends. As they get more serious about esports, they join larger gaming communities. When they find a gaming community, they'll meet others who share their passion for playing. Finding fellow gamers is the first step.

The easiest place to look is close to home. Local gaming events give gamers a chance to compete against a wide variety of players. They share tips and skills and help one another improve. Libraries sometimes host esports events. Esports camps help kids meet fellow gamers. Some towns have esports arenas that can hold thousands of players and fans. One of the largest, Toronto Esports Arena in Canada, holds seven thousand people.

An experienced esports player gives tips to a young gamer wearing a headset.

While some gamers prefer to compete alone, many join teams. A team might invite gamers to join if they're awesome players who have been winning local events. But that's not the only path to team play.

Many schools have esports teams for students. Esports promote interest in science, technology, engineering, and math. To start an esports team at school, gamers just need a few friends and a teacher who can lead.

Students learn about *League of Legends* at an esports training center in Rio de Janeiro, Brazil.

ESPORTS AT SCHOOL

In 2020, the University of North Carolina Wilmington began offering an esports program. Students can learn about gaming, streaming, and careers in esports.

Playing esports on a team in middle school or high school could lead to playing on a college team. There are 175 colleges and universities in the US with varsity esports programs. They give students the chance to play in tournaments and even offer scholarships.

Teammates from the University of Toronto wave to fans at the College League of Legends Championship.

CHAPTER 4

READY TO COMPETE

WHEN GAMERS JOIN COLLEGE ESPORTS TEAMS, THEY ALREADY HAVE A LOT OF GAMING EXPERIENCE. Most college players have been competing for years. They play because they love video games. It's fun to make friends with others who share the same interests. And they enjoy playing for their schools. But many college esports players have bigger dreams. They want to go pro.

Scouts are always looking for players to join pro esports teams. They don't limit their search to college players. Scouts scan the internet, searching for standouts to add to their rosters.

If you're really good at a popular esports game, a scout could ask you to try out for a team.

Gamers who want to join pro teams try to grab the attention of scouts. They stream their play so scouts can see them in action. They jump into online chats with scouts and reach out with questions on social media. Most importantly, they show up for open trials where they have the chance to prove they belong on a pro team.

Teams from Germany (*left*) and the United States (*right*) take the stage at a 2021 esports event in Berlin, Germany.

Members of esports teams wear the same uniforms to create a spirit of unity and teamwork.

Esports events have different rules depending on the game. But there are some rules players almost always have to follow. Harassment and bad behavior are not allowed at official esports events. Dress codes tell players to wear team gear and avoid T-shirts with offensive words and pictures.

Other rules ban the use of cell phones and digital devices during events. They could be used to cheat. Athletes betting on their own games is also off-limits. Esports players earn cash the honest way—by winning it! And there's a lot of money to win. The largest prize pool so far was at The International 2021, an esports tournament in Bucharest, Romania. Gamers competed for more than $40 million.

An esports team celebrates a win at a big event.

As esports become more popular, prizes for the biggest events will grow even larger.

THE OPPORTUNITY OF A LIFETIME

In 2021, TSM wanted *League of Legends* star Hu Shuo-Chieh to play for them. The US esports team offered the player from Taiwan $6 million for a two-year contract. He agreed, but not just for the money. He was excited to take on new challenges in the US.

Can you picture yourself playing esports for cheering fans? At every level of competition, you can improve your gaming skills. You might win at a local event and move on to play in a major tournament. Your fans could include friends, family members, other gamers, and esports followers all around the world. Some of them—such as friends and family—are probably already in your corner. They're eager to see you succeed in esports.

With a lot of practice, you could become a famous esports superstar.

Success doesn't have to mean winning. Esports events are fun and exciting no matter how they end. Jump in as a gamer or just follow your favorite players to have fun with esports!

GLOSSARY

AD: short for *advertisement*

GAMER: a person who regularly plays computer or video games

INCLUSIVE: open to everyone, not limited to certain people

MUSCLE MEMORY: the ability to repeat and improve a muscle movement through practice and repetition

ROSTER: a list of the people on a team

SCHOLARSHIP: money a student receives to help pay for school

SCOUT: a person who searches for talented performers and athletes

STREAM: to watch or transmit online content such as video or music

VARSITY: the top team at a school

VIRTUAL: existing online, not in the real world

LEARN MORE

Esports.com
https://www.esports.com/en

Gregory, Josh. *History of Esports*. Ann Arbor, MI: Cherry Lake, 2020.

National Association of Collegiate Esports
https://nacesports.org/

National Esports Association
https://nea.gg/

Nicks, Erin. *Esports Competitions*. Minneapolis: Abdo, 2021.

Waxman, Laura Hamilton. *The Business of Gaming*. Minneapolis: Lerner Publications, 2021.

INDEX

PHOTO ACKNOWLEDGMENTS

Image credits: Riot Games/Getty Images, p. 4; PixelsEffect/E+/Getty Images, p. 6; RyanKing999/iStock/Getty Images, p. 7; MoMo Productions/DigitalVision/Getty Images, p. 8; adamkaz/E+/Getty Images, p. 9; Roman Kosolapov/Shutterstock, pp. 10, 27, 28; Phiromya Intawongpan/E+/Getty Images, p. 11; Niloo/Shutterstock, p. 12; mihailomilovanovic/E+/Getty Images, p. 13; PonyWang/iStock/Getty Images, p. 14; xavierarnau/E+/Getty Images, p. 15; Three Spots/iStock/Getty Images, pp. 16, 23; Gorodenkoff/Shutterstock, p. 17; South_agency/E+/Getty Images, p. 18; Bertrand Guay/AFP/Getty Images, p. 19; Mauro Pimentel/AFP/Getty Images, p. 20; Josh Lefkowitz/Stringer/Getty Images Sport/Getty Images, pp. 21, 22; Christoph Soeder/picture-alliance/dpa/AP Images, p. 24; Red Bull/AP Images, p. 25; Yaroslav Astakhov/iStock/Getty Images, p. 26; wera Rodsawang/Moment/Getty Images, p. 29.
Design elements: Tuomas A. Lehtinen/Moment/Getty Images; sarayut Thaneerat/Moment/Getty Images.
Cover: Christoph Soeder/AP Images (top); Roman Kosolapov/Shutterstock (bottom).